CULTURAL COMPETENCE WORKBOOK

The Key to Loving One's Neighbor

DEE STOKES

Copyright © 2022 Dee Stokes
All rights reserved. Printed and bound in the United States of America.

No part of this book may be used or reproduced, stored in a retrieval system, or transmitted in any form or by any means, electronic, mechanical, photocopying, recording, or otherwise, without the prior written permission of Dee Stokes, except for brief quotations included in a review of the book or embodied in articles.

The scanning, uploading, and distribution of this book via the Internet or via any other means without the permission of the publisher is illegal and punishable by law.

Please purchase only authorized electronic editions and do not participate in or encourage electronic piracy of copyrighted materials. Your support for the author's rights is sincerely appreciated.

Cover Design: Janie Lee
Interior Design: Janie Lee
Published by: DSM Kingdom Publishers

Cultural Competence Workbook: The Key to Loving One's Neighbor. Dee Stokes. First Edition.
ISBN: 978-1-5136-9416-0

TABLE OF CONTENTS

Foreword	5
Introduction	7
Session 1: Historical/Cultural Context	**8**
Aspects of Biblical Culture	8
Summary & Reflection Questions	15
Session 2: Contemporary Practical Theology	**18**
Summary & Reflection Questions	23
Session 3: 21st Century Missional Ecclesiology	**25**
Summary & Reflection Questions	29
Session 4: Cultural Intelligence (CQ)	**32**
Background and Research	32
4-Factor Model of Cultural Intelligence	34
Incarnational Cultural Intelligence (Pandemic Style)	36
Cultural Intelligence as a Spiritual Discipline of Relinquishment	38
Summary & Reflection Questions	41
Individual/Group Exercises	41
Session 5 Cultural Values (CV)	**44**
Summary & Reflection Questions	52
Individual/Group Exercises	53
Session 6 Unconscious Bias	**56**
Summary & Reflection Questions	61
Individual/Group Exercises	61
Conclusion: Cultural Intelligence as Hybridity	**66**
Reflection Questions	72

Appendices — 74
  A. Answer Key — 74
  B. CQ/CV Action Plan — 75
  C. Unconscious Bias Action Plan — 78
  D. Ways to get to know your neighbor's cultural background — 80

References — 81

Figures — 85

- Bible quotations from ESV unless otherwise noted

FOREWORD

Part of my life's work, other than loving God, loving people, worshipping God, and making disciples, is teaching/training and communicating about culture and specifically Cultural Intelligence. I have researched it, written a whole dissertation on it, taught it, trained folks, and now I am writing this workbook about it.

This workbook is for anyone who loves Jesus and wants to serve Him by loving one's neighbor as themselves. Specifically, it is for your ministry, church, organization, family, and business. Neighborly love can only exist if one understands their neighbor's culture. We live in a world torn apart by the sin of racism. I do not have time to address that sin in this workbook, however, I believe understanding culture, being culturally conscious and sensitive, and applying Cultural Intelligence will lead to the byproduct of reducing racism in America and consequently in the world. This can only be done by celebrating our differences, which will unify us as the people of God. Cultures vary even within ethnic groups. A focus on this can and will facilitate better relationships with those around us and will benefit our communities, churches, organizations, and society as a whole.

This workbook is to be done in small groups as a class or meeting. Each session provides questions for reflection and/or group exercises. This is NOT to be done alone. Each session will increase in content, in assignments, and go deeper in reflection, so dig deep and leave no stone unturned in your discussions. Utilize this workbook over eight (8) sessions or longer, and journey with me as we explore biblical, theological, and ecclesiological implications of culture and take a deep dive into Cultural Intelligence (CQ), cultural values, and unconscious bias in order to better understand and place ourselves, as THE CHURCH, in a better position to love and care for our neighbor.

INTRODUCTION

Culture is simply the way we do things. It includes our norms, values, mores, behavior, and traditions. Culture is everywhere…in every city, nation, state, country, and organization. It can be felt, heard, and seen. The Merriam-Webster Dictionary defines culture as "the beliefs, customs, arts, etc., of a particular society, group, place, or time: a particular society that has its own beliefs, ways of life, art, etc.: a way of thinking, behaving, or working that exists in a place or organization (such as a business)." The American Heritage Dictionary of the English Language defines culture as "the totality of socially transmitted behavior patterns, arts, beliefs, institutions, and all other products of human work and thought." Peterson (2004) posited that culture is "what people think, what they do, or how they feel" (p. 17).

Culture may also include ideas, symbols, and values. There are so many varied definitions, but they all underline the importance of all things in society that make up the individual with exception of an emphasis on or specific mention of spirituality and faith. These are vital proponents of life. Lastly, "culture includes those values, ways of relating and ways of looking at the world that its members share and that provide the framework for all communication" (deSilva, 2000, pp.17-18).

SESSION ONE: HISTORICAL/CULTURAL CONTEXT

Some scholars have spent their lives studying the historical/cultural context of the Bible because of its significance and we, as the Church, cannot downplay culture in our society when it was so very important in the Biblical text. Historical/cultural context refers to the 'background.' It refers to what is going on behind the scenes and in the lives of the characters. Background is vital to understanding any Biblical story as well as the stories of our neighbors. Duvall and Hays (2005) wrote that "historical/cultural context relates to just about anything outside the text that will help you understand the text itself" (p. 100). This may be very interesting to a novice Bible reader. One must understand what is outside of the text to understand what is inside the text. If we do not understand Biblical culture, we will then impart our own ideas, norms, mores…culture into the text. Also, we must understand what is outside, around, underneath, in the past and present of our neighbor to really understand, reach, and minister to them! When studying the Bible and gaining background knowledge, we try to research the characters, the writer of the book, the biblical audience, customs, symbols, word meanings, and anything at all that can help us navigate through and understand the pericope fully. Our focus in this chapter is on the historical/cultural context of the Bible and the importance of knowing the culture of the Bible and our own culture today.

Aspects of Biblical Culture

There are many aspects of Biblical culture that could be highlighted, but this chapter focuses on just a few. Biblical culture included, but was not limited to, an honor/shame society and language. Jesus spoke Aramaic and Hebrew, and the Old Testament autographs were written in Hebrew and the New Testament in Greek. Not everyone attended school or was able to read, write, or speak multiple languages. Biblical culture also included politics, social elements, education, patronage, patriarchy, and societal roles.

To begin our look at biblical culture, we must begin with Jesus. Jesus lived in and by the culture, respected and modeled culture, and also spoke against some aspects of culture. Jesus chose the way of shame in order to be honored. Dying by crucifixion was the most degrading type of death. Deuteronomy 21.23 even speaks to death on a tree being a curse of God. Yet Jesus emptied Himself out and chose the way of a slave in order to receive honor and glory (Philippians 2.7).

We see Jesus responding to the Pharisees in a term called "challenge-riposte." One group or individual is trying to shame another group or individual publicly in an effort to honor themselves. The Gospels are laden with examples of "challenge-riposte" where the Pharisees and other religious officials are trying to shame Jesus in front of large crowds, but to no avail (Matthew 15; Matthew 19.3-9; Mark 15; Luke 20.20-26; John 8.3-11).

Women played a great role in the biblical culture, but were treated as second class citizens. Their voices did not count. They existed in private spaces, while men stood out front. Women were to avoid talking with men in public. They congregated mostly with women outside their families, and their identities were found in their fathers or husbands.

Even how one mourned was a custom in the biblical culture. In the New Testament, there were professional mourners like those outside Jairus' daughter's room in Mark 5.38-39 and Luke 8.52-53. The Old Testament is replete with examples of customs that everyone practiced during mourning. They cried out loud, fasted, put ashes on their head, shaved their heads, and/or tore their clothes (Genesis 37.34; Joshua 7.6; Esther 4.1; Job 1.20; Ezekiel 27.30; Daniel 9.3). And Isaiah consoles mourners by stating the mourners will obtain "beauty for ashes, the oil of joy for mourning, and the garment of praise for the spirit of heaviness" (Isaiah 61.3, KJV). These practices were primarily performed by the Israelites, but the other nations also had certain customs and practices during those times that we will not delve into here.

Honor/Shame

The Biblical culture was one of honor/shame. The Ancient Near East and the Middle East of today were/are shame/honor-based cultures. "In shame cultures, people are more likely to choose right behavior on the basis of what society expects from them" (Richards & O'Brien, 2012, p. 116), not according to right/wrong or the rules. Saving or preserving face is a constant thought in an honor/shame culture. Here in America, we live in more of a guilt-ridden culture. Our guilty consciences cause us to do right. Not so in an honor/shame culture. Scripture is laced with this, but one example is King David with Bathsheba in II Samuel 11-12. Without going too deeply into the story: David, who was married, summoned Bathsheba, who was also married, slept with her, and she became pregnant. Not until Nathan the prophet spoke of this to David was he cognizant that everyone in the palace knew of his affair, and he was ashamed of it. It was not his guilty conscience that made him repent and write Psalm 51. Rather, it was more of a way to "save face" in this type of culture/society. As Westerners, our thinking is much different, but again, we live in a guilt-ridden culture and not the same culture as the Bible.

Honor can be achieved, bestowed upon you, or ascribed at birth. It is a relational aspect. For instance, a married couple maintaining fidelity would be honorable and infidelity, dishonorable. Also, children honor their parents with their behavior so not to shame the family.

Although we live in a guilt type of culture, honor in the American Church can be a fascinating phenomenon. deSilva (2000) posited, "the privatization of religion in the West-the widely shared conviction that an individual's religion is a private matter not to be discussed openly, much less challenged-contributes greatly to the social pressure that fosters pluralism and trammels evangelism" (p. 85). Cultural diversity enriches our churches and lives together as the community of God. We must be careful not to embrace uniformity, but to embrace difference. Different values…different customs…different norms.

Church Culture Today

Throughout this book, the word CHURCH will be mentioned. When CHURCH is mentioned, I am referring to the body of Christ and not just people who gather weekly in a building called a church. We are THE CHURCH in our everyday positions as pastors, presidents, teachers, salespeople, custodians, and the like. THE CHURCH is everywhere, and these concepts are for THE CHURCH universal and NOT just those who are paid to serve in a building/organization called a church.

Ephesians 4 is deemed the chapter explaining five-fold ministry gifts: apostle, prophet, evangelist, pastor-teacher. What we fail to either realize or emphasize at times is that the Ephesian church was multi-ethnic/multi-cultural. Not only was it so in its membership, but also in the leadership…hence the mentioning of five-fold ministers. In Acts 15, the Jerusalem Council met to discuss Gentile membership in the church. The Jews did not require Gentiles to be circumcised nor adhere to their strict dietary customs. This was a major turning point for the church and made it multicultural. The Ephesian church was very culturally diverse and unified. Jews and Gentiles unified in God's Church. It was radical then and is still now because of the homogeneous nature of individual churches. But, although individual churches remain homogeneous, the makeup of Christians looks very different.

According to Tennant (2007), "the typical Christian is no longer an affluent, white, British, Anglican male about forty-five years old, but a poor, black, African, Pentecostal woman about twenty-five years old" (p. 17). There are theological and ecclesiological implications here. Ignoring these would be very costly for the Church. Globalization has played a significant role in society, and that includes the Church. The Gospel is theologically, geographically, and culturally translatable (Tennant, 2007). We should know the trend now that Christianity is growing in Latin America and exploding in Africa and Asia. The Global South has become the center of Christianity. Not only that, immigrant communities are growing in the United States. When immigrants go to other countries, they bring their values, culture, mores, norms, and behaviors. They do not just toss them at the border. This is not reason to be alarmed. This, my friends, is reason to celebrate. We must celebrate what God is doing and how He is moving to unite us as one people to find and present a Church, His Church, without spot or wrinkle (Ephesians 5.27).

Dr. Soong-Chan Rah's *The Next Evangelicalism: Freeing the Church from Western Cultural Captivity* challenges the white Western Church to become aware of how Evangelicalism has been held captive by its predominantly white cultural identity and history. He rightly suggests that immigrant, ethnic, and multiethnic churches are better prepared to adapt to the complexities and realities of this time than the individualistic and materialistic Western and American churches. (Bean, 2014, p. 56)

As America grows with more people of color and other cultures, we will become the wise sages of the future that carry on the legacy of God's Church. As we open up to learn from all people, we will unite in ways we never could have imagined. Church reimagined…

Chimamanda Ngozi Adichie, a Nigerian novelist, in her TED Talk, "The Danger of a Single Story," warns us not to shape our opinions of others on a single story or a single thought of them. She posited, "show a people as one thing, as only one thing over and over again and that is what they become" (Adichie, 2009). Growing up, Adichie was a part of a middle-class family who lived well and even had domestic help living in their home. When she came to America, her roommate "assumed" she was poor, along with some other assumptions. When making assumptions based on stereotypes, history, or even family/friend associations, we miss out on what is important, and we totally miss the uniqueness of the person. Adichie also said, "the problem with stereotypes is not that they are always untrue, but they are incomplete, they make one story the only story" (Adichie, 2009). Luke 7.36-50 is a good example of this. As Jesus is looking at the woman and really seeing her, Simon only sees a single story…a sinful woman. Jesus sees so much more. We must be willing to step out and see more of who our neighbor really is and not base our opinions on a single story. Knowing our neighbor's culture will benefit the Church in more ways than we can put into words. Keep reading and continue on with Session One workbook reflections…

NOTES

SESSION ONE SUMMARY

- To truly understand the Bible, one must know the historical/cultural context or background of the Bible. This is also true when understanding our neighbor.

- Peterson (2004) posits that culture is "what people think, what they do, or how they feel." (p. 17).

- The Biblical culture was one of honor/shame.

- The typical Christian is no longer an affluent middle-aged white male, but a Black Pentecostal young woman.

- Chimamanda Ngozi Adichie, a Nigerian novelist, in her TED Talk, "The Danger of a Single Story," warns us not to shape our opinions of others on a single story or a single thought of them. She posited, "show a people as one thing, as only one thing over and over again and that is what they become" (Adichie, 2009).

Historical/Cultural Context: Questions for Reflection

NOTE: Remember all reflection questions and exercises in this workbook are to be done in a group or groups.

Take this simplified cultural awareness self-assessment, then answer the questions below (Please be honest & go with your first thought)

Question	Agree	Neutral	Disagree
1. I love to travel to different cultures	☐	☐	☐
2. I am very open-minded	☐	☐	☐

Question	Agree	Neutral	Disagree
3. I am flexible	☐	☐	☐
4. I am aware of other cultures when I come in contact with them	☐	☐	☐
5. I am culturally sensitive	☐	☐	☐
6. I think my culture is the best	☐	☐	☐
7. I would never live in another country	☐	☐	☐
8. I speak another language	☐	☐	☐
9. I would love to learn to speak another language	☐	☐	☐
10. I have traveled outside of my country	☐	☐	☐

1. What did you think of this self-assessment?
2. Did it make you more aware of your own cultural awareness?
3. What steps might you take to improve your cultural awareness?
4. Take a moment to reflect on your local church, ministry, family, business.
5. How would you define their cultural awareness?

NOTES

SESSION TWO: CONTEMPORARY PRACTICAL THEOLOGY

I had a Theology professor once say, "you are a theologian if you think about God and the things of God." Therefore, we are all theologians, and all of us possess many "theologies" about God, things of God, and how they pertain to God. Kellemen (2014) posited, "theology is practical and relevant, that truth is for life, that God's Word is robust, real, raw, relevant, and relational" (p. 17). Practical theology in the 21st Century continues to look very different from one context to the other. Practical theology consists of the religious practices we do and reflect upon in our everyday lives (not just in the Church--this is key) that fully embrace our theological notions (what we think about God and the things of God). The reason I stress "everyday lives" is that I believe in a Gospel and theology that are lived out practically. It is lived out at work, school, play, and at rest. It is not just something we do when we enter a building called a church or when we organize a meeting called a ministry. It is lived out every single day of our lives. How we interact with everyday people, in everyday situations, how we relate to God in those situations and with those people is indeed practical theology in praxis, not just in theory. Practical theology became an academic initiative in order to develop theories to guide pastors/leaders in praxis.

Branson and Martinez (2011) deem practical theology to be a process from "experience to reflection and study, and then on to new actions and experiences… praxis" (p. 40). Reflection, in my mind, may be the missing piece. How often and how much time do we spend really reflecting, almost meditating, on process? How often do we reflect on how and why we do things? How often do we reflect on the values and assets of our communities and not just on their needs? The process that Branson and Martinez (2011) have intimated is a constant one. It is a necessary one. It is an essential one.

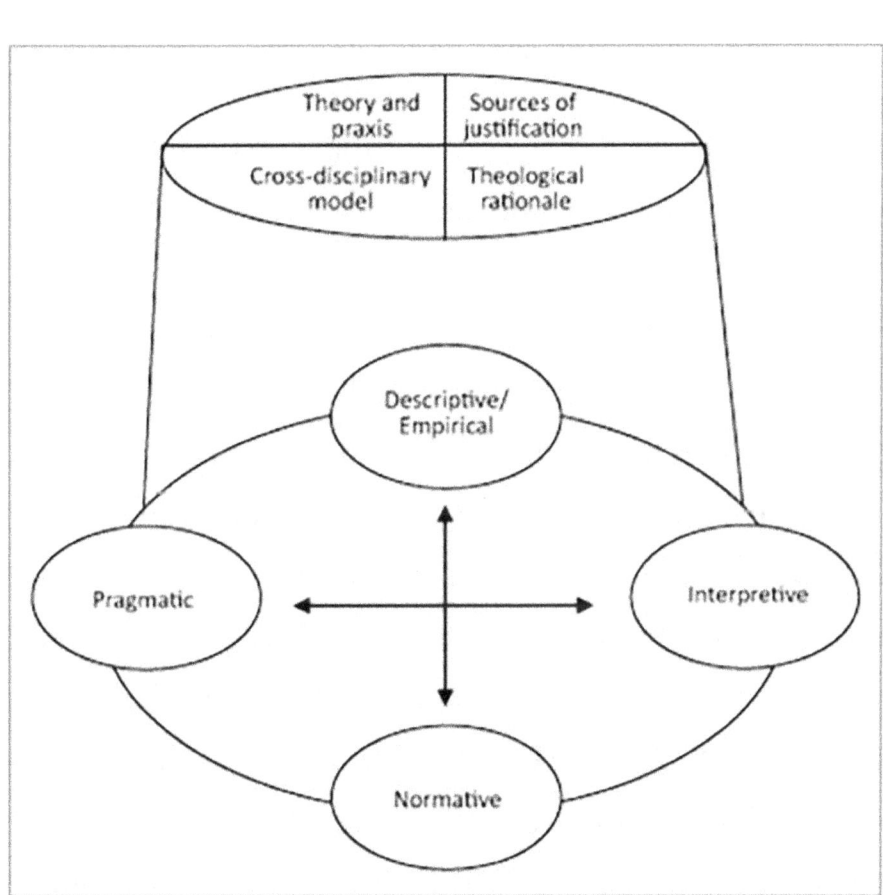

Source: Osmer, R., 2005, *The teaching ministry of congregations*, Westminster/John Knox, Louisville, KY

FIGURE 1: Metatheoretical issues in practical theology.

Another approach for one to consider when discussing contemporary practical theology is in Figure 1. Osmer (2011) explains the following in the diagram above:

1. Theory-praxis may include social practices, theology, and/or philosophy to make decisions about how best to practice.

2. Sources of justification utilizes what many call the Wesleyan Quadrilateral-Scripture, reason, personal experience, and tradition.
3. Theological rationale is based on the theological convictions of the theologian.
4. Models of cross-disciplinary work brings two or more fields together.

This last example is where I would like to land this chapter. Cross-discipline sounds much like cross-cultural to me. Cross-discipline is bringing more than one discipline together to define a problem and create a solution or to make decisions. Using this concept as a metaphor, cross-cultural contemporary practical theology refers to bringing multiple cultures and people to the table to make decisions on how to do practical ministry. This may or may not be based on common theological experience or convictions, but becomes a shared experience where all can benefit. When I think along these lines, I think of fresh expressions of church. Fresh expressions are those expressions of Church that become incarnational and live outside of the church building .

In Kelly Bean's (2014) book How to Be a Christian Without Going to Church: The Unofficial Guide to Alternative Forms of Christian Community, fresh expressions of church abound. The author refers to herself as a "non-goer." This would be someone who was previously entrenched in the church, taught, studied, pastored, tithed, showed up every week, you name it, but left the church because they were seeking more. The book is chock full of examples of fresh expressions and how each one is geared toward the community at large and the folks who gather together weekly, monthly, etc. It speaks of pubs, gardening, Beit Midrash (a house to search for meaning), communities who speak openly about finances in an effort to help everyone live within their means, neighborhood seminaries, farming projects, women's theology groups, you get the picture. The reason Bean's (2014) book intrigues me so much is that it is very practical and shows us that we need to seek after the non-goers as much as we do the unchurched and unbeliever. How will we reach them if we don't indulge in their culture?

NOTES

SESSION TWO SUMMARY

- Practical theology consists of the religious practices we do and reflect upon in our everyday lives (not just in the Church—this is key) that fully embrace our theological notions (what we think about God and the things of God).
- Reflection is a key component of practical theology.
- Reflection leads to process (theory) that leads to praxis (action).
- Cross-cultural contemporary practical theology refers to bringing multiple cultures and people to the table to make decisions on how to do practical ministry.

Contemporary Practical Theology: Questions for Reflection/Exercises

1. Write down the things that you think about God (compile a big list with your group).
2. Write down some of the "religious" practices your church, ministry, family, or business does (compile a big list with your group).
3. How would you bring your practices/processes to life (praxis) in your community?
4. Would having a multicultural group of people making decisions in your church, ministry, family, or business have benefit? How so or how not so?
   a. How will you incorporate a multicultural team in your work?

NOTES

SESSION THREE: 21ST CENTURY MISSIONAL ECCLESIOLOGY

WE HAVE TAUGHT PEOPLE HOW TO LOVE THE CHURCH, BUT NOT HOW TO LOVE JESUS AND HIS PEOPLE!

The aforementioned statement may be bothersome. Some children who were raised in the church and relied heavily on relationships within the church have turned away in recent years. The reason is that we were raised to love the church, and when the "church" (really the people of the church) lets us down, we are disappointed and turn away. However, whether we love the church or are pleased with the church or not, we are called to love Jesus and His people. A missional ecclesiology should point us always to Jesus and those around us.

Missional sounds like such a serious and otherworldly kind of word. It sounds like something you go to Africa or Asia to do, but not something the Church does within our own country (I live in the U.S.). However, if the Church understands the sent-ness of God and that we are a sent people (John 17.18), we embrace the fact that we are ALL missionaries (Matthew 28:19–20; Mark 16:15–18; Luke 9:23). The Church can go further and explain that we are strangers, foreigners, not at home, traveling through until we get home after we have completed our MISSION (Philippians 3.20; I Peter 2.11-12). A missional ecclesiology should begin with knowing and loving Jesus, then knowing and loving the people Jesus created in His image.

Ecclesiology is defined in many ways, but the first step equates to seeing, loving, and responding to God and others around us. We first must 'see' others to be able to love and respond to them and their needs. 'Seeing' is far greater than just a mere glance. It is more of a gaze. What can I really and truly see when I stare at God and others? I mentioned Luke 7.36-50 in session ONE. The dialogue is with Jesus and Simon concerning the 'sinful' woman who was right there in the room with them. Here is a portion of that dialogue:

> Then He turned to the woman and said to Simon, "Do you see this woman? I entered your house; you gave Me no water for My feet, but she has washed My feet with her tears and wiped them with the hair of her head. You gave Me no kiss, but this woman has not ceased to kiss My feet since the time I came in. You did not anoint My head with oil, but this woman has anointed My feet with fragrant oil. Therefore, I say to you, her sins, which are many, are forgiven, for she loved much. But to whom little is forgiven, the same loves little." (vv.44-47, NKJV)

While talking to Simon, Jesus was looking/gazing/staring at the woman. He asked Simon if he saw this woman. But it seemed to be a deeper ask. Did he see her for who she really was or just as a sinful woman who had interrupted their party? Did he see the Imago Dei in her? When we as the Church go into our communities as sent ones, what do we see? Do we always see people who need us to feed, provide shelter, give money to, or do we see people in the image of God, who are just like us...who want to belong, feel loved, and want others to really 'see' them?

The Church (ekklesia) as a called-out group is not just to be a place where people gather. Rather, it is a place to gather and equip people to be on mission, hence the term missional ecclesiology. The Church is not a building. The Church was not meant to be an institution. The Church is who we are as a people following Jesus, and not just where we go or what we do. The Missio Dei should influence our churches and ourselves. Have churches lost this most important concept? Silberman (2019) posited,

…the nature and purpose of the local church are to be shaped by the missional character of God; Father, Son and Holy Spirit. However, even where God's missional nature is recognized, ecclesiological convictions can profoundly impact the ministry of the local church, to the extent that mission is not even considered part of its purpose. (p. 62)

Hence the reason God's Church needs a missional ecclesiology from top to bottom in order to love and serve the differing cultures in and around the Church. The Church is a sending organism engaged in mission at home and abroad. She is shaped by the mission of God and engaged with the world. A missional ecclesiology helps The Church love their neighbor more effectively and profoundly.

NOTES

SESSION THREE SUMMARY

- God sent Jesus, and we are sent to be missional in the earth.
- A missional ecclesiology should begin with knowing and loving Jesus, then knowing and loving the people Jesus created in His image.
- A true ecclesiology begins with us seeing, loving, and responding to God and others around us.
- The Church is not a building or where people gather, it is a called-out group (ekklesia) who are on mission for God.
- A missional ecclesiology helps the Church love their neighbor more effectively and profoundly.

21st Century Missional Ecclesiology: Questions for Reflection

1. How is God moving in your neighborhood, community, and town/city?
2. Where is God moving in your neighborhood, community, and town/city?
3. Is your church, ministry, family, business a witness/missionary in your context?
4. How is your church, ministry, family, business being a witness/missionary in your context?
5. How has your church, ministry, family, business embraced other cultures as a part of your strategy to being missional?
6. Reflect upon a time in the life of your church, ministry, family, business when witnessing (evangelism) and missions was at its all-time high.
   a. How did that feel?

    b. How was that accomplished?

    c. Who was involved?

7. Where will you go from here?

NOTES

SESSION FOUR: CULTURAL INTELLIGENCE

Cultural Intelligence (CQ) is the ability to effectively operate in intercultural settings. Soon Ang and Van Dyne (2008) in their article, "Conceptualization of Cultural Intelligence" defined CQ as "the capability to function effectively across various cultural contexts (national, ethnic, organizational, generational, etc.)" (p. 3). One other definition to consider is CQ is "an individual's capability to function and manage effectively in culturally diverse settings" (Ang, Van Dyne, Koh, Ng, Templer, Tay, & Chandrasekar, 2007, p. 336).

Cultural Intelligence is not just about race or ethnicity. Diverse settings, intercultural settings, and cultural contexts occur in many dynamics within ethnicities, nations, communities, organizations, etc. Therefore, Cultural Intelligence can be an effective tool in every area of society, work, business, government, and the Church!

One's Cultural Intelligence can be measured and can change over time. I highly recommend taking an assessment in the area of CQ and also in the area of Cultural Values. These assessments can give one insight into where one stands in these areas. Cultural Intelligence is a very important concept for the whole of society and I am excited to present this construct to you.

Background & Research

Back around 2011 or so, I abruptly stopped researching emotional intelligence and switched over to cultural intelligence. Mind you, I was two-plus years into finishing my doctorate, but it was the best decision I could have ever made. This concept is life changing. If you embrace it, it will make you want to learn more and simultaneously satisfy your curiosity for other cultures. In my own research, I have found that leaders who are highly culturally intelligent experience less burnout and are more transformational (Stokes & Szapkiw, 2014). This is what we need in our Church leaders. The Church needs leaders who are resilient, enthusiastic, culturally sensitive, healthy, and transformational.

Hofstede (1980) and Schwartz (1994) began this journey of studying cultural intelligence. Hofstede studied IBM employees and found cultural values of power distance, uncertainty avoidance, individualism-collectivism, and masculinity-femininity, long term orientation, and indulgence (See summary for definitions). Later Schwartz added the concept of culture and how we fit into and dominate (or not). It has now gone on to be studied by many and expanded over the years to include four dimensions with each dimension having subdimensions and as well as exploring the ten cultural values.

Having a knowledge of Cultural Intelligence not only helps to navigate one's own culture, but allows one to adapt to many different cultures.

Groves and Feyerherm (2011) posited that leader cultural intelligence (CQ) should be understood and is far more important to understand than emotional intelligence or other leadership traits, behaviors, or characteristics. Their research indicated that leaders with high levels of CQ had followers who were more loyal and the leader's CQ was stronger when teams were more culturally diverse. They also found that followers rated their leaders high in performance and this rating far outweighed the effects of a leader's emotional intelligence. (Stokes & Szapkiw, 2014, p. 50)

Cultural Intelligence helps us to connect outside our own culture (Ang, et al., 2007; Earley & Ang, 2003). Groves and Feyerherm (2011) emphasized that leaders had high Cultural Intelligence when they were among teams that were more culturally diverse. We need leaders in the Church who are highly culturally intelligent and sensitive to the needs of those they lead. Cultural Intelligence helps us understand and love our neighbor on a greater level.

4-Factor Model of Cultural Intelligence

"Cultural Intelligence is a multidimensional construct targeted at situations involving cross-cultural interactions arising from differences in race, ethnicity, and nationality" (Ang, et al., 2007, p. 336). Cultural Intelligence (CQ) also requires an individual to adapt effectively to new cultures (Earley & Ang, 2003; Stokes & Szapkiw, 2014). The four-factor model of Cultural Intelligence includes the dimensions of motivational (drive) CQ, cognitive (knowledge) CQ, metacognitive (strategy) CQ, and behavioral (action) CQ. All Cultural Intelligence subscales can of course be measured and can change over time.

Motivational (CQ DRIVE). CQ drive expresses our interests (intrinsic vs. extrinsic) and self-efficacy or confidence in functioning effectively in intercultural situations. These three (self-efficacy, intrinsic, and extrinsic interests) are the subdimensions of CQ drive. "Motivational CQ [drive] is the capability to direct attention and energy toward learning about and operating in culturally diverse situations" (Rockstuhl, Seiler, Ang, Van Dyne, & Annen, 2011, p. 827). Individuals highly skilled in this area are characterized by effort and energy and have a strong desire to interact and experience others from differing cultures.

Cognitive (CQ KNOWLEDGE). CQ knowledge touches on our knowledge of similarities and differences between cultures. We may have a general knowledge, and there may be specific things we know about other cultures like socioeconomic systems, mores, norms, values, etc. Individuals highly effective in this area are "open-minded and understand other cultures' systems, culture itself, economics, and legality" (Stokes & Szapkiw, 2014, p. 41). There are four subdimensions when it comes to CQ knowledge. They include values and norms, business attitudes, sociolinguistics, and leadership. According to my personal CQ report, values and norms may include "social interactions and religious beliefs;" business refers to "economic and legal systems;" sociolinguistics refer to "language and communication;" and leadership refers to "managing people and relationships across cultures" (Stokes 2021 CQ report).

Metacognitive (CQ STRATEGY). CQ strategy is the thought process and planning stage of Cultural Intelligence. Now that we have some knowledge, how will we further understand diverse/intercultural settings? Ethnocentrism plays a part in this stage as we often view other cultures through the lens of our own culture and think that our culture is superior. It is important to be aware of this and not allow it to inhibit our effectiveness. Strategy also focuses on processes, and those high in this area spend an inordinate amount of time thinking about other cultures. "Metacognitive CQ [strategy] is an individual's level of conscious cultural awareness during intercultural interactions" (Rockstuhl, et al., 2011, p. 827). The three subdimensions of CQ strategy include checking, planning, and awareness.

Behavioral (CQ ACTION). CQ action measures one's ability to adapt in intercultural settings. How do you adjust when encountering other cultures? It is important to realize that speech, body language, and verbal and non-verbal cues play an important role in CQ action. These factors are the three subdimensions of CQ action (non-verbal and verbal cues and speech acts). "Behavioral CQ [action] includes interpersonal skills and social skills exhibited during cross-cultural encounters" (Stokes & Szapkiw, 2014, p. 42, paraphrasing Ang, et al., 2004).

Incarnational Cultural Intelligence (Pandemic Style)

Incarnational Cultural Intelligence is a term I coined. My definition is *"being effective in intercultural settings while dwelling among people outside the walls of the church."* Jesus was incarnational (John 1.14). He dwelt among the people. The late Eugene Peterson wrote, "He moved into the neighborhood" (The Message Bible). I Corinthians 9.20-22 highlights Incarnational Cultural Intelligence. Paul wrote,

> When I was with the Jews, I lived like a Jew to bring the Jews to Christ. When I was with those who follow the Jewish law, I too lived under that law. Even though I am not subject to the law, I did this so I could bring to Christ those who are under the law. When I am with the Gentiles who do not follow the Jewish law, I too live apart from that law so I can bring them to Christ. But I do not ignore the law of God; I obey the law of Christ. When I am with those who are weak, I share their weakness, for I want to bring the weak to Christ. Yes, I try to find common ground with everyone, doing everything I can to save some. (New Living Translation)

Combining these two terms (incarnational and Cultural Intelligence) seems appropriate for what God commanded us to do in the Great Commission. We enter into others' worlds (cultures) so we can understand them and their cultures without disobeying God in order to influence, equip, love, help, and empower them for Christ. If we as the body of Christ are still interested in ALL souls being reconciled to God and obtain eternal salvation, then we will be committed to Incarnational Cultural Intelligence.

Cultural Intelligence has always been important for the Church. However, only recently (within the last fifteen or more years) has this concept been introduced and emphasized globally. Biblical scholars understand the significance of culture when interpreting the Biblical text. Culture played a major role in customs, traditions, how people were chosen, family affairs, etc. within the entire Bible. Why would 21st Century scholars, Church leaders, and world leaders not honor or choose to understand the cultures surrounding them in order to be more effective in their roles? Interesting question, isn't it? As we have survived and some have thrived during the pandemic, many things have changed, and I pray we have learned much, but it seems we still have a way to go in truly loving our neighbor as ourselves. Being incarnational and having a high level of Cultural Intelligence can move us closer to fulfilling the Great Commandment.

As we progress in the 21st Century, it has become increasingly noted that Cultural Intelligence can help churches become more vital by simply reaching more people. Multiethnic and multicultural churches are an ever-increasing entity all over the United States. Michael Emerson (2008) found in his research that in the United States in the 1990s, there were 6% multiethnic churches, and it was expected to rise to 20% by 2019. Garces-Foley (2010) found that "protestant churches with 1000 weekly attendance was three times more likely to be multiracial in 2007 than in 1998, and evangelical churches of the same size were five times more likely in 2007." (p. 64). Although the latter stats are considered what we would deem a "megachurch" in America, the same can apply to smaller congregations, as Baylor University's study showed that one in five Americans attend a racially mixed place of worship. This would mean that the number of congregants doubled from 1998 to 2012. If the trends continue to rise, we will see more and more unity in the body of Christ concerning ethnicity, race, and culture. Let's embrace this now!

Cultural Intelligence as a Spiritual Discipline of Relinquishment

I mentioned Jesus emptying Himself out in Philippians 2.7 in the Historical/Cultural session. I want to return to that thought. Here is a blog post I rewrote in January 2021 for Luther Seminary's Faith + Lead website about Cultural Intelligence as a spiritual discipline of relinquishment:

Cultural Intelligence is the ability to interact and work effectively in intercultural settings or contexts. These may include family structures, organizations, regions of the country, ethnicities, etc.

Spiritual disciplines are designed to increase our spiritual formation so that we can become more Christ-like. These can include disciplines of abstinence like fasting and chastity or disciplines of engagement like worship, study, or prayer. There are many spiritual disciplines.

Relinquishment is letting go of issues and things that may hinder us from something, but doing so with hope, assurance, and joy. We pray prayers of relinquishment to let things go that bother us, detract us from what God has called us to, and then allow God to work those things out for us. We put our full trust in Him to do so.

I was teaching a course at our Fresh Expressions Resilient Church Academy, and one of my students asked a very unique, thought-provoking question. "What if we viewed Cultural Intelligence as a spiritual discipline of relinquishment?" I was floored (in a good way) by his suggestion. It made me contemplate and of course, write. What if…? What if we let go of our perceptions, and notions and stereotypes about other cultures? By the way, when I say other cultures, I don't mean those outside of your sphere…I mean those differing cultures that are right in your face! The ones in your church, next door to you, on the job, and in your city. People you know and see each and every day. What if we let go of preconceived notions and maybe even let go of some of our strongly held cultural norms and traditions in order to better understand and appreciate our neighbor? What if...?

Philippians 2.7 reads, "have this mind among yourselves, which is yours in Christ Jesus, who, though he was in the form of God, did not count equality with God a thing to be grasped, but emptied himself, by taking the form of a servant, being born in the likeness of men" (ESV). The King James Version reads that He made "Himself of no reputation," meaning to make void, to empty, to abase, to lay aside His equality with God so He could be like us. Selah...

What would I give up, empty out, lay aside in my culture to embrace another's culture? Surely, I would need to step out of my comfort zone in order to do this. Surely, I would need to decide if my values, mores, norms, traditions were even appropriate and if they were excluding others from being in my circle. What was the Kingdom culture of Jesus? He preferred the poor, outcast, lame, blind, women, and others as He poured into them for three and a half years before making the ultimate sacrifice on the cross. What would you give up to understand your neighbor better? What would the world look like if we (individuals and the Church) relinquished our hate, negative opinions, incorrect notions, etc. about other cultures? I, as an eternal optimist, seem to think the world would be a better place, God's Church would flourish, and things would look oh so different. Much thanks to my student for making me contemplate this thought. As you finish this blog, you think as well how you can be the change God seeks in the world!

NOTES

SESSION FOUR SUMMARY

- The 4-factor model of Cultural Intelligence (CQ) includes Motivational CQ [Drive], Cognitive CQ [Knowledge], Metacognitive CQ [Strategy], and Behavioral CQ [Action].
- Incarnational CQ is *'being effective in intercultural settings while dwelling among people outside the walls of the church."*
- Cultural Intelligence might be seen as a spiritual discipline of relinquishment.

Cultural Intelligence: Questions for Reflection/Group Exercises

1. What are your thoughts on Cultural Intelligence as a spiritual discipline of relinquishment? Take a moment to reflect.
2. How do you think you fit into the Cultural Intelligence picture? Rate yourself.
3. How will you use this information within your own life? Church? Ministry? Family? Business?

4-Factor Model of CQ

Instructions: Match 4 Dimensions on the left with all that apply on the right

A. Strategy
B. Knowledge
C. Drive
D. Action

1. Effort & Energy _____
2. Verbal & Non-Verbal _____
3. Open-minded _____
4. Understands Cultural Systems _____
5. Flexibility _____
6. Spend Time Thinking _____
7. Strong Desire to Interact _____
8. Conscious Awareness _____
9. General Knowledge _____
10. Interpersonal & Social Skills _____

11. Focuses on Processes _____

12. Strong Sense of Self-Efficacy _____

NOTES

SESSION FIVE: CULTURAL VALUES

Values can be summed up as the things we hold dear to us. Things we think are important. Priorities that influence our daily lives, work, play, family relationships, church, etc. According to Russell (2001), "Values affect leader behavior, values constitute the foundation of servant leadership & leader values may be the underlying factors that separate servant leaders from all other leadership types" (p.76). Servant leadership can simply be looked at as leadership that focuses on others. As servant leaders, we attend to the needs of other people. However, it is much more than just feeding dinner to a number of people on Monday nights. Having a cultural conscience can help us to be true servant leaders who know, understand, and empathize with our neighbors and not just treat them as people we need to help. We are to work and serve *with* others, not *for*.

Kouzes and Posner (1993) said leadership practices and processes are amoral, and I will add that the carrying out of said practices and processes can be moral or immoral based on whether the leader is moral or immoral. Russell (2001) added that the leader's morality/values influence the organization as noted in Russell's (2001) abstract that the literature states "values affect leader behavior as well as organizational performance." (p.76). We think, have a worldview, and lead based on our values. Leadership matters, but if leaders are self-centered, then how could they lead others and organizations effectively? Values-based leadership is ever evolving in business and in other entities. Values affect behavior, reasoning, ethics, and judgment, and the stronger the values, the more ethically a leader behaves (Hughes, et. al, 1993). Values can be influenced by culture and other contexts. It is a incorrect to think that leaders' attitudes, behaviors, and values do not impact an organization. Indeed, they do, and organizational transformation cannot occur without leader transformation.

There are ten Cultural Values that exist globally. There are also ten cultural clusters where these values are likely to be seen, not exclusively, but in large numbers. As a disclaimer, cultural values are seen everywhere, and one cannot generalize a particular culture, people, or region. Even if seen in great numbers within clusters, values can differ among individuals, organizations, groups, etc. There is no right or wrong answer to what you value culturally. Understanding each other's values is vital in working toward loving our neighbors.

10 Cultural Clusters

NOTE: "The Countries are not the clusters themselves, they are places where you are likely to see the cultural clusters" "The Curious Traveler" by David Livermore

Cluster	Sample Countries
Anglo	Australia, Canada, New Zealand, United Kingdom, United States
Arab	Bahrain, Egypt, Jordan, Kuwait, Lebanon, Morocco, Saudi Arabia, United Arab Emirates
Confucian Asia	China, Hong Kong, Japan, Singapore, South Korea, Taiwan
Eastern Europe	Albania, Czech Republic, Hungary, Mongolia, Poland, Russia
Germanic Europe	Austria, Belgium, Germany, Netherlands
Latin America	Argentina, Bolivia, Brazil, Chile, Columbia, Costa Rica, Mexico
Latin Europe	France, French-speaking Canada, Italy, Portugal, Spain
Nordic Europe	Denmark, Finland, Iceland, Norway, Sweden
Southern Asia	India, Indonesia, Malaysia, Philippines, Thailand
Sub-Saharan Africa	Ghana, Kenya, Namibia, Nigeria, Zambia, Zimbabwe

—Chart adapted from *The Curious Traveler* by Dr. David Livermore

Ten Cultural Values

1. Individualism vs. Collectivism (Theme: Identity)

In an individualistic culture, being true to the individual is the ultimate goal. "In a collectivist culture, the most important entity is the community…not the individual" (Richards & O'Brien, 2012 p. 9). Richards and O'Brien (2012) go on to write that in a collectivist culture, "a person's identity comes not from distinguishing himself from the community, but in knowing and faithfully fulfilling his place" (p. 97).

How do we think of ourselves? Do we often see ourselves as individuals, or as a group, family, neighborhood, or community? This cultural value emphasizes individual rights vs. relationships and group goals. You can determine an individualist vs. collectivist by the way they work. One likes to work independently and the other with a group. *How can knowing this value benefit your church, ministry, family, business?*

- Example of an individualistic culture: Germanic Europe
- Example of a collectivist culture: Confucian Asia

2. Power Distance (Theme: Authority)

This value is measured in terms of low or high-power distance. According to the Cultural Intelligence Center's definition of power distance, it is a preference for hierarchical (high) leadership vs. egalitarian (low) leadership. Some value formalities in language, titles, chain of command, and status (high-power distance). Low-power distance advocates need to be empowered, and high-power distance advocates need to be addressed in formal ways and given feedback one on one. *How can knowing this value benefit your church, ministry, family, business?*

- Example of a low-power distance culture: Anglo (includes U.S.)
- Example of a high-power distance culture: Latin America

3. Uncertainty Avoidance (Theme: Risk)

How much are we willing to take risks (low vs. high)? This value measures how flexible we are in uncertain situations. How can we adapt and change vs. trying to reduce as much anxiety and uncertainty as possible? High-uncertainty avoidance cultures would like to see emphasis put on planning, and low-uncertainty avoidance cultures tend to be OK with ambiguity. *How can knowing this value benefit your church, ministry, family, business?*

- Example of a low-uncertainty avoidance culture: Nordic Europe
- Example of a high-uncertainty avoidance culture: Latin Europe

4. Cooperative vs. Competitive (Theme: Achievement)

This value has nothing to do with winning or losing. It involves whether results are preferred to be achieved collaboratively or competitively; within relationships or individually task oriented. *How can knowing this value benefit your church, ministry, family, business?*

- Example of a cooperative culture: Sub-Saharan Africa
- Example of a competitive culture: Anglo

5. Time Orientation (Theme: Time)

Time orientation is the focus one prefers to have on immediate results (short-term) vs. results several months or years down the road (long-term). Success now or success later. How can knowing this value benefit your church, ministry, family, business?

- Example of a short-term Time Orientation culture: Eastern Europe
- Example of long-term Time Orientation culture: Confucian Asia

6. Context [Direct vs. Indirect] (Theme: Communication)

Direct/low context is explicit and direct communication, whereas indirect/high context is more harmonious with the emphasis on not making others look bad (saving face). Direct communicators use precise words and try to be very clear in their communication. Indirect communicators use other cues and pay close attention to body language and their surroundings. *How can knowing this value benefit your church, ministry, family, business?*

- Example of a Direct Context culture: Anglo
- Example of an Indirect Context culture: Arab

7. Being vs. Doing (Theme: Lifestyle)

This value emphasizes quality of life. Being cultures tend to work less hours, relax more, and take long vacations. Doing cultures tend to work more (even at home when not at a formal job) and emphasize high productivity. *How can knowing this value benefit your church, ministry, family, business?*

- Example of a Being culture: Latin America
- Example of a Doing culture: Germanic Europe

8. Universalism vs. Particularism (Theme: Rules)

Do you feel as though there are standards and rules that everyone should abide by (universalism)? Or should those rules/standards be viewed differently and applied differently based on relationships and situations (particularism)? *How can knowing this value benefit your church, ministry, family, business?*

- Example of a Universalism culture: Anglo
- Example of a Particularism culture: Southern Asia

9. Expressiveness [Neutral vs. Affective] (Theme: Expressiveness)

This value emphasizes hiding emotions (neutral) vs. expressing them (affective). Neutral cultures may be difficult to read because they hide their feelings well, and affective cultures may be misunderstood because they express their feelings openly. How can knowing this value benefit your church, ministry, family, business?

- Example of a Neutral culture: Eastern Europe
- Example of an Affective culture: Latin Europe

10. Monochronic vs. Polychronic [Linear vs. Non-Linear] (Theme: Focus)
This value measures how one focuses their attention. Are you a multitasker or not? Monochronic/linear cultures focus on one thing at a time while polychronic/non-linear cultures tend to shift their focus and do multiple things (multitask). How can knowing this value benefit your church, ministry, family, business?

- Example of a Monochronic/Linear culture: Nordic Europe
- Example of a Polychronic/Non-Linear culture: Sub-Saharan Africa

Note, in general, collectivism, high power distance and high uncertainty avoidance tend to be positively correlated [have a positive relationship] (Basabe & Ros, 2005; Purohit & Simmers, 2006; Matusitz, & Musambira, 2013). As relationships between variables go, when one goes up and the other goes up, this corresponds to a positive relationship. When one goes up and the other goes down, the relationship would be negative. Collectivist cultures tend to have high-power distance and high uncertainty avoidance.

In a simpler form, Peterson (2004) organized cultural values into five scales (see figure 1). They include equality vs. hierarchy, direct vs. indirect, individual vs. group, task vs. relationship, and risk vs. caution. These simplified scales equate with the above cultural values and may be easier for society to comprehend and pay attention to. In my opinion, these five scales would be fairly easy to trace in any society in the world. Equality vs. hierarchy then becomes power distance. Direct vs. indirect is how we communicate with each other. Individual vs. group is our identity and corresponds to individualism vs. collectivism. Task vs. relationship is a theme for being vs. doing, which in turn equates to our lifestyle and how we relate to others and work. Risk vs. caution would be equal to uncertainty avoidance and measure how much risk a person is willing to take.

EQUALITY	VS.	HIERARCHY
DIRECT	VS.	INDIRECT
INDIVIDUAL	VS.	GROUP
TASK	VS.	RELATIONSHIP
RISK	VS.	CAUTION

Figure 2: Adaptation of Peterson's (2004) 5-scale Cultural Values

NOTES

SESSION FIVE SUMMARY

- The Hofstede Insights website (www.hofstede-insights.com) defines each dimension as such:

  - **Power Distance:** "the extent to which the less powerful members of institutions and organizations within a country expect and accept that power is distributed unequally."

  - **Individualism:** "the degree of interdependence a society maintains among its members."

  - **Masculinity-femininity:** "The fundamental issue here is what motivates people, wanting to be the best (Masculine) or liking what you do (Feminine)."

  - **Uncertainty Avoidance:** "the way that a society deals with the fact that the future can never be known."

  - **Long term orientation:** "how every society has to maintain some links with its own past while dealing with the challenges of the present and future."

  - **Indulgence:** "the extent to which people try to control their desires and impulses."

- Values can be summed up as the things we hold dear to us. Things we think are important. Priorities that influence our daily lives, work, play, family relationships, church, etc.

- There are ten cultural clusters where we see dominant cultural values.

- The ten cultural values include:
  - Individualism vs. Collectivism (Theme: Identity)
  - Power Distance (Theme: Authority)
  - Uncertainty Avoidance (Theme: Risk)
  - Cooperative vs. Competitive (Theme: Achievement)
  - Time Orientation (Theme: Time)
  - Context [Direct vs. Indirect] (Theme: Communication)
  - Being vs. Doing (Theme: Lifestyle)
  - Universalism vs. Particularism (Theme: Rules)
  - Expressiveness [Neutral vs. Affective] (Theme: Expressiveness)
  - Monochronic vs. Polychronic [Linear vs. Non-Linear] (Theme: Focus)
- Not everyone within a culture, country, or nation has all the same cultural values.

Cultural Values: Questions for Reflection/Group Exercises

1. How can knowing these cultural values help your leadership in The Church, your ministry, family, business?
2. How will you apply these cultural values?
3. Reflect on these Cultural Values and think how you can help your church, ministry, family, business understand them better.
4. What will you do with this knowledge now?

Based on the Ten Cultural Values, how would you rate yourself?

(Refer back to the chapter, then place a check or X by the values that correspond to you)

1. How do these ratings affect you?
2. How will you use them in your interactions with others?

NOTES

SESSION SIX: UNCONSCIOUS BIAS

According to the University of California, San Francisco Office of Diversity and Outreach, "bias is a prejudice in favor of or against one thing, person, or group compared with another usually in a way that's considered to be unfair. Biases may be held by an individual, group, or institution and can have negative or positive consequences" (https://diversity.ucsf.edu/resources/unconscious-bias). Conscious bias (or explicit bias) and unconscious bias (or implicit bias) are the two types of biases. Explicit biases are a conscious set of behaviors and attitudes by individuals, groups, or organizations, while implicit or unconscious biases are unintentional, subconscious thoughts. The UC San Francisco Office of Diversity and Outreach also note that, "biases, conscious or unconscious, are not limited to ethnicity and race. Though racial bias and discrimination are well documented, biases may exist toward any social group. One's age, gender, gender identity physical abilities, religion, sexual orientation, weight, and many other characteristics are subject to bias" (https://diversity.ucsf.edu/resources/unconscious-bias). The university also emphasizes on their website that

> Unconscious biases are social stereotypes about certain groups of people that individuals form outside their own conscious awareness. Everyone holds unconscious beliefs about various social and identity groups, and these biases stem from one's tendency to organize social worlds by categorizing. *Unconscious bias is far more prevalent than conscious prejudice and often incompatible with one's conscious values.* Certain scenarios can activate unconscious attitudes and beliefs. For example, biases may

be more prevalent when multi-tasking or working under time pressure. (https://diversity.ucsf.edu/resources/unconscious-bias)

Everyone has biases. This should not be difficult to believe or to understand. We may be very good people who love and respect everyone, but we still have biases. We have biases toward food, people, places, cultures, ethnicities, skin color, body size, our favorite stuff, you name it, we ALL have biases. This is the reason I emphasized the statement above that "unconscious bias is often incompatible with one's conscious values." Our unconscious bias comes from unintended subconscious thoughts about people, places, and things. It is extremely important that we recognize that we all have it (bias), and by understanding it better, we can combat some of those unconscious thoughts and bring them to the forefront of our mind to consciously deal with them. Bias is not always negative. Evaluating someone too positively is a form of bias. Bias shapes everything: education, church, the criminal justice system, relationships, business, customer service, you name it. It is everywhere. Once bias becomes conscious, we can then combat and manage it. Cultural Intelligence is a key factor in managing bias.

Covering

Covering, a form of unconscious bias, is a technique used by those who are uncomfortable about sharing personal and/or professional information with others in the workplace, church, or another environment. Most people who cover some aspect of their lives do not feel comfortable or safe enough to disclose certain things. One example of this is a wife and mother who covers the fact that she works outside the home and her husband stays at home with the majority responsibility of raising the children. Depending on what part of the United States one lives in, this can be a very difficult decision to make. For some, this seems to be a light thing, but for others, it weighs heavily on their minds. There are other things people cover, like sexuality, birthplace, family, legal battles, where one grew up, and so on. How can the Church, your ministry, family, or business address this issue and make others feel welcomed, accepted, and loved?

Microaggressions

Dr. Maura Cullen (2008) wrote a quite intriguing book called 35 Dumb Things Well-Intended People Say. It is basically a book of microaggressions and explanations for each. I highly suggest you read it. Before I started doing work in the area of unconscious bias, I read this book and it has shaped some of my thoughts in this area. Microaggressions, a form of unconscious bias, are things people do or say that are derogatory and based on ethnicity, gender, age, or other factors. For instance, when one sees a well-dressed Black man getting out of a luxury vehicle, one's mind tends to wander about what profession he might be in. Did your mind wander as you read that? That example is a typical microaggression. And there are many others. Read the book…

So, imagine someone walks into your church or business who looks, smells, acts, dresses, talks differently than you and everyone else in the room. What is your first reaction? I have to share this funny but sad story with you. I had a Sunday off and went to support a pastoral colleague of mine on his first Sunday at his new church. I was the only Black person there beside those on the worship team. I sat down close to the front so he could see me, and one of the assistant pastors, a white female (for context) came over to greet me. She asked me what brought me here today. I chuckled inside and kept my composure. I should have said I came to meet with Jesus, but I politely ignored her remark and stated that I was a friend of the pastor. Shortly after, he greeted me and eventually introduced me to the entire congregation. Friends, this is a true story. I don't tell it to make you cringe (or maybe I do), but I absolutely believe that the assistant pastor did not mean any harm, but these unconscious biases are so embedded in the everyday fabric of our lives that we must combat them.

NOTES

SESSION SIX SUMMARY

- "Unconscious bias is far more prevalent than conscious prejudice and often incompatible with one's conscious values." (https://diversity.ucsf.edu/resources/unconscious-bias)
- Cultural Intelligence is a key component in managing unconscious bias.
- Everyone has bias. Everyone has been a victim of bias. Everyone has made a biased decision.
- Covering is a technique used by those who are uncomfortable about sharing personal and/or professional information with others in the workplace, church, or other environment.
- Microaggressions are things people do or say that are derogatory and based on ethnicity, gender, age, or other factors.
- Covering is a way to avoid unconscious bias, and microaggressions are forms of unconscious bias.

Unconscious Bias: Questions for Reflection [These can be done individually and as a group]

1. Do you have unconscious biases? YES NO
2. Have you been the recipient of others' biases? YES NO
3. Can unconscious bias can be controlled? YES NO
4. Does everyone have unconscious biases? YES NO

Types of Bias include: _____ _____

What is covering, and what are some strategies to combat covering?

_____
_____
_____
_____

What are microaggressions, and what are some ways to combat microaggressions?

_____
_____
_____
_____
_____

Matching
Match the numbered responses to the alphabetical responses

1. Unconscious Bias | 2. Covering | 3. Microaggression | 4. Favor bias

A. We should hire him because he goes to my church _____

B. I have Black and Asian friends _____

C. My father is in prison and I won't tell anyone _____

D. I know what you are feeling _____

E. I am not sure we can hire a Baby Boomer _____

F. My best friend recommended this person to be our worship pastor_____

G. I hide my disability _____

H. We need to hire a female in this position, the previous males did not work out _____

Unconscious Bias: Group Exercises

Role Play Scenarios: Take these scenarios and role play them with your team

1. *Two male managers in the organization are about to meet with a female candidate for a position. They both have spoken with her on the phone and feel good about hiring her. The final step is the in-person interview. The female candidate comes in, interviews well, spends about thirty minutes with the two male managers, and heads out. The following is discussed after her departure: "I did not know she was so large and out of shape," one manager said. "How will she ever do the job?" The other manager asks, "Why are you so concerned about her weight? This job does not require strenuous activity?"*

    QUESTIONS TO PONDER:
    A. What kind of bias is this?
    B. How do you feel about this situation? (BE HONEST)
    C. Have you been in or seen this type of situation before?

* After you play this out, go back and create a separate role play on what should have been done instead and discuss with the group.

2. *There are three candidates for the engineering position. One is a white millennial male with tattoos all over his body, another a Muslim American woman, and the other is a middle-aged white female.*

    QUESTIONS TO PONDER:
    A. Which one do you hire and why? (You cannot say you don't have enough information…go with the first choice that popped into your head)
    B. Was your choice biased?
    C. If I told you the millennial male was the most qualified and was hired,

what would you think? (First thing that pops into your head)
D. How can you rectify your bias in this case and discuss further with the group?

3. *An attractive Black female comes for a job interview. She is a finalist. She looks great and presents herself well for the interview. There is only one exception. The interviewers and several folks in the office were "offended" by her hairstyle and claimed it was not professional enough for their workplace.*

   QUESTIONS TO PONDER:
   A. What kind of bias/discrimination is this?
   B. Who (what people group) mostly makes up the rules when it comes to hair in the workplace?
   C. How would you handle this situation?

4. *A friend wants to go to dinner. They invite you along and want you to meet another person (a friend of theirs) and invite them along as well. The other friend happens to be Native American. You immediately assume you cannot offer the Native American guest a drink because of the many stereotypes you have heard. So, instead, when the waiter comes, you order water for the entire table and tell the waiter no one will be drinking tonight.*

   QUESTIONS TO PONDER:
   A. What kind of bias/discrimination is this?
   B. How should the friend who invited everyone to dinner respond?
   C. What would you have done differently if given the chance for a do over?

NOTES

CONCLUSION: CULTURAL INTELLIGENCE AS HYBRIDITY

The homogeneous unit principle was thought to help churches grow. The principle states that churches grow when the congregants are racially and culturally the same (homogeneous). It goes a step further to imply that the congregants in these churches actually respond to the Gospel more effectively as well. How is this working for us today with the numbers increasing in terms of diversity? Acts teaches us that God grew the Church (which was culturally and ethnically diverse at the time). Specifically, in Acts 2.47 "the Lord added to the Church daily those who were being saved" (NKJV). The Church was vibrant, vital to the community, fellowshipped, broke bread together, prayed together, studied and followed in the Apostles' doctrine and teaching, shared all things in common including their possessions, the Apostles' witnessed about Jesus' resurrection with great power and authority, were favored with grace and more grace, and there was no lack among them (Cf. Acts 2.40-47; 4.32-37). "The missional church framework requires that we deepen our knowledge of our contexts, including ethnicities and cultures, so we can become more capable of wise and effective leadership in our churches" (Branson & Martinez, 2011, p. 67).

The Church is made up of people. You and I joined together to make a difference in this world and in God's Kingdom. Places of worship on Sundays may look segregated. They may not be culturally or racially diverse. People may want to worship with their neighbors or those who are similar to them. What if we stopped fighting that fight and realized that no matter where we worship one day a week, we still need to be culturally and ethnically diverse as the Church, the body of Christ, baptized believers, one Church coming together to do God's will and make a difference the rest of the week. Stocking our churches full of people who look differently is not exactly the point. It would be nice because heaven is diverse, but we need to come together as a people for God and work alongside each other. Once we do that, we then show the world who we really are, and things shift and change in God's favor, and a by-product would be multiethnic and multicultural churches! Honestly, some may think that in homogeneous churches, everyone has the same culture. I would dare write that all churches are multicultural in some way. They may or may not be multiethnic, but I dare step out on a limb and say they are multicultural. Even within ethnicities, there are differing cultures. Differing values, norms, mores, behaviors, etc. Not all people groups act and think alike, so the value of understanding our neighbor's culture increases all the more.

Kenneth E. Bailey, in his 2008 book *Jesus Through Middle Eastern Eyes: Cultural Studies in the Gospels,* mentions that in the Matthean genealogy of Jesus, there are five women mentioned (including Mary, the wife of Joseph). The women beside Mary were Tamar, who birthed a son by her father-in-law Judah, Rahab, the prostitute, who hid the spies in Joshua 2, Ruth, a Moabite, who stayed attached to, Naomi an Israelite, and Bathsheba, who became pregnant by and eventually married King David. But look a little closer at these women and their cultures. "Ruth and Rahab were Gentiles, Tamar was probably a Gentile, and Bathsheba was originally married to a Gentile" (Bailey, 2008, p. 42). Their stories are worth remembering. Tamar was married to Judah's son who died. Because of the cultural practice of Levirate marriage (Deuteronomy 25.5-10), a brother was to marry the deceased sibling's wife and bear children. The second brother married Tamar but refused to have children, so he died. The third brother was too young at the time, so Judah promised Tamar they would marry once he was old enough. That time came and no marriage, so Tamar took it upon herself to dress as a prostitute and seduce Judah, who ended up impregnating her. Scandalous indeed. Rahab was a prostitute, but a God-fearing woman (an oxymoron in American culture) and hid the spies when they came to spy out Jericho. Ruth was married to one of Naomi's sons who died. Ruth chose to stay with Naomi and Naomi's people became her people, and Naomi's God became Ruth's God (Ruth 1.16). They go to Bethlehem at the beginning of the barley harvest and meet up with Boaz, who is a kinsman of Naomi. The rest is history as Boaz and Ruth marry in another Levirate marriage. Bathsheba was the wife of Uriah and she placed herself on her rooftop in order for King David to take notice. David had her husband killed in the line of duty and took her as his wife after it was known that she was with child. The baby died, but the two stayed together and had more children, including Solomon. Of course, Mary is the mother of Jesus and was a saintly, young virgin. Saints and sinners form this genealogy of the women in Jesus' family. Matthew highlighted women, which was taboo in that time, but not just women, people outside of the normal Israelite culture. These "outsiders" became "insiders" and are a part of the lineage of Jesus. This is important to note. Those who may seem like "outsiders" to us in our churches, ministries, families, and businesses are the very ones we need to approach and bring to the "inside."

Hybridity is defined as a mixing or a crossing between cultures. Baker (n.d., 6) posits hybridity is "allowing new patterns of worship and spiritual identity to emerge from the plural and diverse experiences within globalized localities" (p. 6). I believe there is a hybridity in Cultural Intelligence. Cultural Intelligence as hybridity considers the surrounding culture and blends those ways of doing things into the Church. Isn't this what practical theology is? A way of doing/

practicing what we know and believe. A way of being incarnational with our neighbors. Homi Bhabha, a leading exponent of hybridity, developed the idea of the Third Space. These are spaces outside of where one works, lives, plays, and goes to church. Third spaces could be coffee shops, museums, bowling alleys, bars, restaurants, the mall, you name it. In these Third spaces is where we can meet our neighbor, interact, and talk about Jesus, family, business, health, life, and anything else in an effort to be incarnational. These are non-threatening spaces where others visit and hang out. A hybrid space might be a good place for practical theology to take place and where we can know and love our neighbor.

THE CHURCH needs to *know* all it can about people. Loving our neighbor cannot be accomplished if we do not *know* our neighbor. This *knowing* is not on a surface level. It is a deep dive into the life and culture of those we work with, pastor, live with, play with, and cry with. The concepts of Cultural Intelligence (CQ) will help get us on the right track with understanding and loving our neighbor better. As we journey along in this kingdom, don't we want to walk alongside as many people as we can? Get to know as many as we can so they can know the One who "walks with us and talks with us and tells us we are His own?" What are we waiting for?

The final thought here is the Church must be UNIFIED. Unity is the answer. Jesus in John 17 prayed that we would be one. "I do not ask for these only, but also for those who will believe in me through their word, that they may all be one, just as you, Father, are in me, and I in you, that they also may be in us, so that the world may believe that you have sent me" (verses 20-21). Some have stated that there are at least 100 verses on unity in the Bible. For example, I Corinthians 1.10, "I appeal to you, brothers, by the name of our Lord Jesus Christ, that all of you agree, and that there be no divisions among you, but that you be united in the same mind and the same judgment." Philippians 2.1-3 explains,

> So, if there is any encouragement in Christ, any comfort from love, any participation in the Spirit, any affection and sympathy, complete my joy by being of the same mind, having the same love, being in full accord and of one mind. Do nothing from selfish ambition or conceit, but in humility count others more significant than yourselves.

"So then let us pursue what makes for peace and for mutual upbuilding" (Romans 14.19). It is good and pleasant for us to be unified. It is like the oil running down Aaron's beard from his head down to his robe. It is like the dew of Hermon and where the Lord has commanded the blessing, life forever and ever and ever (Psalm 133, *paraphrase mine*). I could go on and on and on and quote more scripture describing the type of unity God has ordained and insisted upon for His Church. Schism is not an option. deSilva (2000) agrees, "the words schismata and erides conjure up images of factions, of ugly rivalry, of breaches of the unity and harmony that is the ideal stare of an honorable family" (p. 218). We are family. We are the body of Christ

It is this author's belief that learning Cultural Intelligence will help in rebuilding relationships within the body of Christ that will last until Jesus returns. My prayer is that through my personal work in this area and with the reading, contemplation, questions, and exercises in this workbook, we will unite now more than ever before. Only as one body can we make a difference that will last for Christ and help us love our neighbors as ourselves!

NOTES

Conclusion: Questions for Reflection

1. Sit for a while and reflect upon what you have read. What images does your mind conjure up about God's Church, your ministry, family, business?
2. What steps will you take now that you have read this book?
3. How can you be a light and make a difference with this information in mind, in and out of your church, ministry, family, business?
4. Why is this important to you personally?
5. Why is this important for your context (family, work, church, etc.)?

Now contiue on with the remainder of the workbook's exercises and add a session or two if needed…

NOTES

Appendix A (Answer Keys)

Answer key to 4-Factor Model of CQ

1. Effort & Energy: C
2. Verbal & Non-Verbal: D
3. Open-minded: B
4. Understands Cultural Systems: B
5. Flexibility: D
6. Spend Time Thinking: A
7. Strong Desire to Interact: C
8. Conscious Awareness: A
9. General Knowledge: B
10. Interpersonal & Social Skills: D
11. Focuses on Processes: A
12. Strong Sense of Self-Efficacy: C

Answer key to Unconscious Bias Matching

A. 4-Favor Bias
B. 3-Microaggressions
C. 2-Covering
D. 3-Microaggressions
E. 1-Unconscious Bias
F. 4-Favor Bias
G. 2-Covering
H. 1-Unconscious Bias

Appendix B

Action Plan for Cultural Intelligence (CQ) & Cultural Values (CV)

NOTE: Action planning should be one of the final sessions of your work together. A prayer session could be included after the action planning work is done.

What goals do you have for utilizing this information?

_____
_____
_____
_____

What challenges do you face in your church, ministry, family, business, and life when it comes to CQ, CV, and multiculturalism?

_____
_____
_____
_____

What opportunities do you have to share this information?

_____
_____
_____
_____

Based on either your perceptions of your own CQ or feedback from a CQ assessment, which one of your strengths can be explored in greater depth?

_____
_____
_____
_____

List 2-3 things you will do in the next 30 days to build relationships outside of your sphere of influence.
_____
_____
_____
_____

How will you attempt to increase your CQ & awareness of CV?
_____
_____
_____
_____

Which factor of CQ are you the weakest in?
_____
_____
_____
_____

How will you address this weakness?
_____
_____
_____
_____

Who will you ask to hold you accountable?
_____
_____
_____
_____

Next Steps:

WHO	WHAT	WHEN	WHERE

Appendix C

Action Plan for Unconscious Bias

How will you utilize this information on unconscious bias?

_____
_____
_____
_____

How will you utilize Cultural Intelligence and Cultural Values to minimize bias?

_____
_____
_____
_____

Name 2-3 things you will do in the next 30 days to minimize bias in your ministry.

_____
_____
_____
_____

How will you measure effectiveness/impact?

_____
_____
_____
_____

Next Steps:

WHO	WHAT	WHEN	WHERE

Appendix D

Ways to get to know your neighbor's cultural background

- Have a meal once a month (virtually or in person) and get to know each other.
- Share things about your lives and personal experiences (take notes after the meeting, if necessary).
- Visit a cultural event together (virtually or in person).
- Interact with a church who is a cultural opposite of you (NOT a pulpit swap, but significant time together).
- Visit a museum together (virtually or in person).
- Ask questions.
- Plan a family vacation with a family of a different culture.
- Do business with a company of a different culture.
- Partner in some way with someone from a different culture.
- Play golf together (what a great way to get to know someone).
- Take long walks together.
- Have a neighborhood cookout or block party and invite everyone on your street to not only eat, but participate in the planning, cooking, and serving.
- Have a neighborhood Zoom meeting and learn about each other's likes and dislikes.
- Celebrate a neighbor's birthday, birth of a child, anniversary, baby or bridal shower (virtually or in person).

References

Adichie, C. (2009, July). *The dander of a single story* [Video]. TedGlobal. https://www.ted.com/talks/chimamanda_ngozi_adichie_the_danger_of_a_single_story?language=en

Ang, S., & Van Dyne, L. (2008). *Handbook of Cultural Intelligence: Theory, measurement, and applications.* M.E. Sharpe.

Ang, S., Van Dyne, L, Koh, C., & Ng, K.Y. (2004). *The measurement of cultural intelligence.* Paper presented at the Academy of Management Meeting's Symposium on Cultural Intelligence in the 21s Century. New Orleans, LA.

Ang, S., Van Dyne, L., Koh, C., Ng. K.Y., Templer, K.J., Tay, C., & Chandrasekar, N.A. (2007). Cultural intelligence: Its measurement and effects on cultural judgment and decision-making, cultural adaptation and task performance. *Management and Organization Review, 3*(3), 335-371.

Bailey, K. E. (2008). *Jesus through Middle Eastern eyes: Cultural studies in the Gospels.* InterVarsity Press.

Baker, C. (n.d.). Hybridity and practical theology: In praise of blurred encounters. *Contact 149,* 5-11.

Basabe, N., & Ros, M. (2005). Cultural dimensions and social behavior correlates: Individualism-Collectivism and Power Distance. *International Review of Social Psychology, 18*(1), 189 225.

Bean, K. (2014). *How to be a Christian without going to church: The unofficial guide to alternative forms of Christian community.* Baker Books.

Branson, M.L., & Martinez, J.F. (2011). *Churches, Cultures, & Leadership: A practical theology of congregations and ethnicities.* InterVarsity Press.

Cullen, M. (2008). *35 Dumb Things Well-Intended People Say: Surprising things we say that widen the diversity gap.* Morgan James Publishing.

Cultural Intelligence Center. www.culturalQ.com.

Culture. *In The American Heritage Dictionary of the English Language.* https://www.ahdictionary.com/word/search.html?q=Culture

deSilva, D.A. (2000). *Honor, patronage, kinship & purity: Unlocking New Testament culture.* InterVarsity Press.

Duvall, J.S., & Hays, J.D. (2005). *Grasping God's Word: A hands-on approach to reading, interpreting, and applying the Bible.* Zondervan.

Earley, P.C., & Ang, S. (2003). *Cultural intelligence: Individual interactions across cultures.* Stanford Business Books.

Emerson, M.O., & Smith, C. (2000). *Divided by Faith: Evangelical religion and the problem of race in America.* Oxford University Press.

England, G. W., & Lee, R. (1974). The relationship between managerial values and managerial success in the United States, Japan, India, and Australia. *Journal of Applied Psychology, 59(4),* 411–419.

Farhadian, C.E. (Ed.). (2012). *Introducing World Christianity.* Wiley-Blackwell.

Garces-Foley, K. (2010). *Multiethnic Congregations.* Center for Christian Ethics at Baylor University. https://www.baylor.edu/content/services/document.php/110977.pdf

Groves, K.S., & Feyerherm, A.E. (2011). Leader cultural intelligence in context: Testing the moderating effects of team cultural diversity on leader and team performance. *Group & Organizational Management, 36(5),* 535-566.

Hofstede, G. (1980). Motivation, leadership, and organizations: Do Americans' theories apply abroad? *Organizational Dynamics,* 9, 42-63.

Hofstede Insights. (2021, April 17). *Country comparisons: Japan.* Hofstede Insights. https://www.hofstede-insights.com/country-comparison/japan/

Hughes, R. L., Ginnett, R. A., & Curphy, G. J. (1993). Leadership: Enhancing the lessons of experience. Irwin.

Kellemen, R.W. (2014). *Gospel-Centered Counseling: How Christ changed lives.* Zondervan.

Livermore, D.A. (2019). *The curious traveler: See the world.* Change your life. Cultural Intelligence Center.

Matusitz, J., & Musambira, G. (2013). Power distance, uncertainty avoidance, and technology: analyzing Hofstede's dimensions and human development indicators. *Journal of Technology in Human Services, 31(1),* 42-60.

Merriam-Webster. (n.d.). Culture. In Merriam-Webster.com dictionary. https://www.merriam-webster.com/dictionary/culture

Osmer, R. (2005). *The Teaching Ministry of Congregations.* Westminster/John Knox.

Osmer, R. (2011). Practical theology: a current international perspective. *HTS Theological Studies, 67(2),* 1-7

Peterson, B. (2004). *Cultural Intelligence: A guide to working with people from other cultures.* Nicholas Brealey Publishing.

Posner, B. Z., & Kouzes, J. M. (1993). Psychometric properties of the Leadership Practices Inventory—Updated. *Educational and Psychological Measurement, 53(1),* 191–199.

Purohit, Y. S., & Simmers, C. A. (2006). Power distance and uncertainty avoidance: across-national examination of their impact on conflict management modes. *Journal of International Business Research, 5(1),* 1.

Richards, E.R., & O'Brien, B.J. (2012). *Misreading Scripture with Western eyes: Removing cultural blinders to better understand the Bible.* InterVarsity Press.

Rockstuhl, T., Seiler, S. Ang, S., Van Dyne, L., & Annen, H. (2011). Beyond general intelligence (IQ) and emotional intelligence (EQ): The role of cultural intelligence (CQ) on cross-border leadership effectiveness in a globalized world. *Journal of Social Issues, 67(4),* 835-840.

Russell, R.F. (2001), "The role of values in servant leadership", *Leadership & Organization Development Journal,* Vol. 22 No. 2, pp. 76-84.

Schwartz, S. H. (1994). Beyond individualism, collectivism: New cultural dimensions of values. In U. Kim, H.C. Triandis, C. Kagitcibasi, S.C. Choi, & G. Yon (Eds.), *Individualism & collectivism: Theory, method, and applications* (pp.85-119). Sage.

Silberman, T. (2019). Un-missional Church? Knox-Robinson ecclesiology and the mission of the local church. *Colloquium 51(2),* 61-76.

Stokes, D.M., & Rockinson-Szapkiw, A. (2014). Cultural intelligence, transformational leadership, & burnout: The 21st Century leader's playbook for understanding the relationship between CQ, TL, and Burnout. Lap Lambert.

Tennent, T.C. (2007). *Theology in the Context of World Christianity: How the global church is influencing the way we think about and discuss theology.* Zondervan.

UC San Francisco's office of Diversity and Outreach.
(https://diversity.ucsf.edu/resources/unconscious-bias)

Figures

Figure 1. Metatheoretical Issues in Practical Theology

Figure 2. Adaptation of Peterson's (2004) 5-scale Cultural Values

NOTES

NOTES

NOTES

NOTES

NOTES

NOTES

NOTES

NOTES

NOTES

NOTES

www.ingramcontent.com/pod-product-compliance
Lightning Source LLC
LaVergne TN
LVHW061216060426
835507LV00016B/1969